The many eyes of beauty wait
for the song of silence
to begin

Sacred Nature Poems

Colin Willcox

Also by Colin Willcox

Selected poems on the deepest experience of Love, reflected in Nature, in the Other and in the longed for unknowable.

Sacred Nature Poems

ISBN: 978-0-9573136-2-0

Published by The Quiet Bell Press

Poems by Colin Willcox

iamcolin55@gmail.com
www.thequietbell.com

Contents

23 the stillness at the centre
24 eventually the flowers fade
25 how every birdsong begins
26 the sea does not grow old
27 dancing without feet
28 a single moment of light
29 what do flowers need
30 another world awaits
31 wingtips painting patterns in the sky
32 the silent voices of the forest
33 at this time of the year
34 keeping the whole world alive
35 nothing else is needed
36 the circle of leaves
37 the choiceless path
38 nothing has been seen before
39 returning to earth
40 to want for nothing
41 approaching wings
42 silence of the birdsong
43 the sound of the bell
44 the sky is just the beginning
45 an undiluted taste
46 the sun knows nothing of the dark

47 before the light
48 sometimes the night flowers
49 time does not need words
50 this is how the Summer ends
51 wet leaves falling from the sky
52 even butterflies need sleep
53 the grasshopper knows
54 the unnoticed silence
55 beyond the senses
56 every corner has its place
57 the dark makes a home
58 have we really seen the swallows
59 everything is here
60 so all this can begin
61 where the daily joys feed
62 how many stars do we need
63 the clouds return to Earth
64 the snail is always perfectly at home
65 the ten thousand shapes of thought
66 beauty changes shape
67 this day is laid to rest
68 life is what happens
69 the stillness where every song begins
70 the silence of truth

1

now is when it all begins
sitting here
breath by breath
right on the edge
of awareness
listening
to everything
and then
deeper
the silence within
nothing
is what it seems
without the words
even air and light
dissolve
all the shapes of separation
jigsaw
into one
filling every form with beauty
in this
fleeting eternity

2

this is what the dawn
awakes to
trees
misty with darkness
and branches wide
with dew-dipped leaves
and damp feathered stirrings
of a new day

a thousand eyes wait
for light to begin
yet shadows too
have their secret places
where songs are born
and unfolded wings
can soar unseen
just as high
as flight in dreams

everything is needed
for this moment
to unfold

3

Who knows
where the path
will find
its moment
of contentment

Sometimes
familiar places
can reveal
the deepest joy
of discovery

and life leaps
beyond the clouds
of assumption
to touch
that clear light
of infinite
appreciation

4

the day returns
everything in its place
trees and stones
barely moved
birds
on their familiar perches

yet every sound is new
every light beam
never seen
this moment's breath
more precious
than the ten million
long forgotten

each thought
fades away
and in between
the one silence
stays the same

5

Light is not the only source
of illumination

Sometimes darkness
can break through
walls of illusion
to give birth
to the root
of awareness

This is how we grow
watering the seeds
of acceptance

until everything gives way
to the flower
of unextinguished
gratitude

6

I know the way the birds sleep
folded
quiet
alone

yet there is a song they keep
for the morning light
and wings
and eyes
very like our own
that wait
like we wait
for every sign of beauty
to sink in

Until we have wings
our hearts will beat
a little faster
in quiet anticipation
of Light
of Life
of Love

and flight
will be as nothing
to what may come hereafter

7

Winter has her flowers
little scented jewels waiting
cold butterflies
to kiss

every day is our season
petals to behold
fallen leaves
of worlds now past
and buds
of newness
to unfold

the shape of things change
within the presence
the changeless
surrenders
in the end

however deep the stillness
the watcher and the listener
the ever present witness
stays the same

8

all the shapes of water
moving
in every liquid being
in the awakening mist
at dawn

rabbits leave footprints on the dew
whilst swans glide
ruffling the pattern
of reflected trees

no one but the heron sees the fish
weaving silver pathways
above the pebbled sand
and breezy trailing weeds
that they call home

we all begin as fish
with secret gills and fingered fins
until we remember
which side of the rippled surface
we were born to breathe

9

even clouds have songs
that fall as rain
or shady shapes
on timeless Summer days

Every tree has its circle of shadow
a refuge from the spotlight
of time
the coolness of rest
whispering the moments
that we forgot to caress

In the listening
there is a long way
between thoughts
only the silence
remembers
to believe

10

the trees have leaves once more
quietly
every branch
is full

Now light has a home again
green things to breathe
flowers
to inspire

new life is here
leaf by leaf
petal by petal
the shape of Spring
reborn
from Winter's deepest shadows

everything is changed
by looking
closer deeper
nothing is the same
when seen
for the first time

11

however far
these spirals of birdsong
merge

even the silences
carry
note by note
secrets
that cannot be heard

this is what the senses are for
to reach beyond the shadows
beyond the light
beyond
every distinction
until the whole world
is pulsating
in ever present
space

12

even meadow flowers know
which way the sun goes
and follow
open limbed
that journey of light

and owls
just as aware
resurrect their life
from the fading of the day
the folding of the petals
the silencing of birds
the merging of the shadows
into darkness
alive and breathing

every movement has a shape
delicate senses
asleep   awake
the trees stand guard
beating hearts
and bird-sized dreams
nestle in their branches

13

this is what she says
this tree
leaning into the light
that surrounds me

that however deeply I gaze
into the river of time
all that is revealed
on the reflecting surface
is the tranquility
that is always here

another breath
of this soft grass
three birds
silhouette the sky
with song
and not even my prayer
can cloud the stillness
of amazement

14

the clouds this morning
the mist
every leaf upon the tree
quiet
all the birds
awake

footstep by footstep
the path is here
and the world converges
to this point

in the momentary peace
this timeless silence
has a language
to be learnt

there is so much more to love
when life
continues
to expand

15

two swans
pulsate the air
condensing time
wing beats
firmly flying home

this is the kind of world we live in
dragonflies
their thousand petalled eyes
shimmering the many suns
fleeting on the morning pond

all of nature is alive
the surrounding trees
so close to silence
lend their momentary reflection

even the stones
gathered in prayer
are dancing with the ripples
of whatever light is

16

the morning light is here
to outshine yesterday's dream

in the expanding stillness
of this moment
from what direction
does tomorrow come

without the speaking voice
of time
everything is
just this

life
within life
galaxies of cells
and every one
is home

17

every leaf awake
the light
the air
and now the rain
begins

these are the moments that matter
witnessing
the birds
weaving the spaces
in between
this song

However wide the circle
all the changing shapes of time
return
raindrop by raindrop
the sky
the earth
are one

18

In time
    the grass grows over
    the walled garden
    that I had tended

In time
    the wild flowers
    scatter their beauty
    and ignore those straight lines
            that I had ploughed

In time
    the earth surrenders
    breaking every pattern
    that my reason
            bestowed upon her

Who knows
what growing thing
is struggling
with imagined droughts
to recreate
    the sacred groves
        we have so casually
            abandoned

19

Suddenly it is now
the trees are full of leaves again
the grass is damp
with early sun
the night
and all her dreams
are nowhere to be seen
the awakening thoughts
forgotten
light
and all the dappled shadows
we dance to
silence
and all the echoing
songs of life
emptiness
full of absent spaces
where memory
refused to lie
listening
even breathing
can be enough
to bring the whole world
to life

20

a deer sits in the long grass
every sense
awake
at ease

listening
to the silence
between the birds
and the trees

watching
for the unfamiliar
the unknown
the unseen

this is where the secrets lie
behind the shadows
before the thoughts
beyond the dream

the deer and I are looking
nothing that is obvious
is ever what it seems

21

the leaves reveal
their butterfly colours
before their short flight
of spiralling
independence

we are all one tree
rooted
in the same soil
even the birds
exalted in their freedom
land feet first
on quiet branches

Everything surrenders
to its place
raindrops find their river
and the mountains
touch the clouds

22

I read the newspapers today
all of them page to page
They didn't mention the cherry pink blossom
or the birch tree
now coming into leaf
or the countless waking beings
calmly brewing
    their early morning cup of tea

They wrote about some shooting in Baghdad
but someone must have heard
the blackbird in the garden
    silencing the dawn

There were three photographs
of a train crash near Moscow
but nothing of the dappled light
clinging
    to the new born leaves of Spring

And don't we sometimes need reminding
of children
finding pebbles on some forgotten beach
and maybe one page for the oceans
and the forests
and the mountains
and for everything
    that does not speak

23

a blackbird
        in a distant tree

a dove in flight

        shadows
                tangled in damp grass

        and where am I

this ever widening spiral
        of outer things
                my senses seem to touch
        evaporate
                in the stillness
                at the centre
                of each dissolving thought

the world and all her colours
                come and go

        here I am
                is everything
                        I need to know

24

eventually
the flowers fade

the butterfly's wing
        folds to dust

even this tree
        firm and wise with years
        will crumble
                without trace

every thought has its memory
sharp and real and true

and yet
second by second by second
        nothing is left
every breath dissolves
        with nothing
                but air
                    to take its place

25

bird nests
        anchored like ships
                in a stormy tree
precious cargo
        secure within the hold
no roof
        but wings
                and warm feathers
        to shield life
                into life

this is the way
        that every birdsong begins
from broken eggs
        and tangled twigs
a miracle
        remembering
                        to sing

26

the clouds know nothing
of time
every shape
evolving
dissolving
into nothing
or one

not even rain has a history
once fallen
the puddles and the rivers
continue to flow

the sea does not grow old
with the passing of the years

wave after wave
everything begins
forever
and ever

27

every day the sun
starts again
another journey of light
to encircle our world

however still we stand
the hours widen and expand
filling every moment
with new senses

nothing stays the same
every chapter
another adventure

even this tree
quietly breathing
her kaleidoscope of leaves
will catch some breeze
dancing
without feet

28

this is how the world begins
all the clouds of thought
give way
to a single moment
of light

in such stillness
nothing
is out of place
everything
is here

and these changes that come
steady as rain
or breathing
weave the flow
of unknowable
perfection

29

what would the flowers say
of Winters gone
of last week's storm
of yesterday
the scent is here today
the air
sunlight
and look a bee
petals open
everything is ready
and complete

what do flowers need
but this constant
moving moment
to be
what else to wish for
to want or to miss
but every atom
inch and second
of this
just this

30

any tree can tell us
how to find the light
even roots need to know
where not to look

this is what we learn
that light is always here
at the beginning
one step at a time
is illuminated
with quiet
softer
resting places
until we leap again

another pool of light
to splash in
another world awaits
our re-creation

31

I count the unseen distance
the soundless spacing
    of the wood pigeon's call
even closed eyes
    measure time
        by memory

in the naked world of flight
    nothing is too delicate
        to hold

birds that once left home
    are now wingtips
        painting patterns
            in the sky

a thousand petals of rain
        and still
    the song begins again
        like nothing else
            exists

32

It is the silent voices of the forest
that I notice most
the ten thousand million growing points
of every tree
unfolding leaf
unfolding flower
unfolding Spring

These are the footsteps I remember
the ones that trace the sound
of growing things
the ones that rejoice
at newborn flowers
and sun-dried wings

That is the world I discover
the busy lives of timeless birds
reminding me
that there is no greater worship
than to marvel
at this day

In such a mood
I am amazed
my every thought is stilled
A living Earth is shaken
by a gentle morning wind

33

At this time of the year
the cherry tree
outside my window
unfolds her infinite petals
of purest white
It is this celebration
of Spring
dancing in the wind
of change
that awakens
the presence in me
Petal by petal
and leaf by leaf
we grow our world
to fit our needs

Flowers are not the only reminders
of our transient nature
yet their fragile beauty
remains long after
I look away
their scent catches me
unaware
just when I thought
they were too small
to care

34

however many journeys
we have lived
and all the roads we think
that we have yet to find
it is only
this breath
that is important
this breath
that keeps
the whole world
alive

the sleeping bird that folds
first her wings
then her eyes
listening
until nothing's left
unheard
breathing
calmness

35

clouds have lives that change
move
from place to place
every moment
new shapes
to be

thoughts are seldom seen
for what they are
spinning their words
into shadows
drifting far away
from the light

looking in the spaces left behind
maybe
nothing else is needed

just the peacefulness
of an empty sky

36

the circle of leaves
pressed tightly wet
upon the grass

the empty tree
still dances
with the breeze
two resting birds
supervise
the grey sky

every tree
has a winter soul
to watch over
long nights
to grow familiar
with letting go
nothing is left out
nothing is alone
the circle
draws us home

37

thank you for the stillness
filling every sound
for the pure calm presence
breathing
whilst all the world
comes rushing by

the senses touch
but do not hold fast
each precious
changing
glimpse of this

thinking has no centre
just a rippling past

letting go
I find the way
open to
the choiceless path

38

the shape of leaves
like fingerprints
a thousand stars
at night
blades of grass
the passing cloud
every grain of sand
the same
at first glance

moment by moment
the world awakes
to our attention

nothing has been seen before
by eyes that look
beyond the veil
of expectation

39

time does not change anything
even footprints in the snow
melt
to what they were before
and the broken fragments
of this storm-torn tree
return
to earth

however much memory
pretends to know the past
a bucketful of thoughts
dissolve
with every glimpse
of this
unchanging stillness

expanding awareness
until everything
lies within

40

at this time of day
first light
every leaf awake
new shadows
step by step
leave my path
unchanged

I know that it can be enough
to live one moment
by itself
to breathe
as deeply as this tree
to touch
unfiltered beauty
in the air
and want for nothing
to begin

41

spiders follow patterns
that maybe million year old ancestors
once calculated
in joyful inspiration

who knows what came first
this handful of dust
gathered tightly
into life
or this sacred world
spinning light
in pools
of swirling webs

every thread is connected
every cell is linked
and somewhere near the centre
we sense
approaching wings

42

waiting
for the words
to end
for the silence
of the birdsong
and the whisper
of the breeze
ruffling these patient trees

one more breath
and all the world is here
awake and alive

It is only the senses that need me
to be aware
all the thoughts of heaven
do nothing
but compare

and when I come to make my plans
I know that that shall be
my purpose
like all the other creatures
to be a good companion
to our Earth

43

as the sound of the bell
fades away
into silence

what is listening

who is waiting
for the senses
to begin

with every breath
the world
is new

with every breath
life
comes in
the open door

44

the sky and all her clouds
are just the beginning

distant lights
as far as we can see
do not end

how big does this universe have to be
for one blackbird
to fill this field
with song

and those who live
with tiny wings
amongst the scented pollen
collect galaxies
of unseen seeds
that light the way
for honeyed bees
to chart
their jewelled
journey home

45

yesterday's trees
are still here
and yet the light
that shook their leaves
is nowhere to be seen

everything is different

however much we link
memory
with a new unfolding
of an unexperienced
nowness
everything is new

that is how the butterfly
awakes
every flower worth
an undiluted taste

46

the sun knows nothing
of the dark
that silences these trees

an owl
echoes its aloneness
while unheard wings
prey
on unseen life
hurrying home to sleep

and now the rosy tips of dawn
arise
the hunger of a new found day
unfolding wings
and soft-toed limbs
listen

one song is all it takes
and as the light comes flooding in
the air
the air itself
the air we do not see
the air the air awakes

47

Light
and before the light

space

waiting

to be illuminated

emptiness
is where it all begins

breathing has to start
before form
takes shape

we are all linked
to that initial
spark

48

Sometimes the night flowers
forget to close
and the butterflies can't sleep

one touch of the scent
of the moonlit rose
and the dreamer awakes
the senses
unfold

This is not just another day
life is here
fleeting and exposed

Everything is waiting
for this moment
to be welcomed
home

49

in years long past this tree
seeded
and one tiny root
fed and watered
a fragile shoot
reaching for the light

now a million leaves rejoice
atop a trunk, branched and bold
solid in its certainty
seasoned
balanced
like stone

right here in the stillness
cool light surrounds me
I listen to the shadow
echoing in the quietude

time does not need words
within the moment
everything is heard

50

the swallows
weaving the air
and the evening light etched
on spider webs
the trees
shift and jostle
shimmering the breeze
flies cloud the water
ripples
where the dragonfly
bounces

this is how the Summer
ends

warm wings
bellies full of memories
eyes
a perfect circle
mirror the setting sun

51

after the rain
wet leaves
hold the memory

one by one
footprints
tell a history

however far the journey
we have not moved
wind
and the bending tree
returns

we are all
explorers
of the moment

wet leaves
falling
from the sky

52

breathing
alive
even butterflies
need sleep

the colours of flight
wing tip
to wing tip
fold
like silenced lips
or tired hands
at prayer

today keeps pace
only with itself
and in that peace
comes the joy
of nothing
to compare

53

the rocks
and all the miles of soil
beneath our feet
the sky
that the clouds
can barely reach

and time
how deep how wide
how fast
how slow

what is there to measure
in the spaciousness
between

the grasshopper knows
how to sing
with its knees

54

the forest at dawn
the birds awake
awake
and light
made real
by every outstretched leaf
and shape and shade
of countless things
as seen

and yet
between the trees
an ocean of this
unmapped space
the birds and I
breath in

it is the unnoticed
silence
that gives meaning
to the song

55

every butterfly that comes
from the sunlit garden
to the unexpected darkness
of the grove
brings the scent of flowers
and the sound of wings
closed to any other world

We all feed on flowers
and the fruit of days
filled with little wisdoms
and delights

In a world that comes and goes
the senses have so much more
to discover
yet beyond the senses
right at the centre
before even breathing
has a name
the butterfly
is always at home

56

every corner has its place
every shape
every colour
finds its way
into the pattern
of today

no piece is ever wasted
however dark
or empty
may be the space

everything
fits somewhere
into the whole

one moment
endlessly
finding itself
with nothing
to withhold

57

the day
fills her cup with light
drop by drop
the waking birds
have one more song
to begin

this is what today is
another reason
to be

all the colours of time
spin past
but now
when the evening comes
it is the dark
that makes a home
to believe in

one by one the shadows merge
all distinctions cease
the hurried day is silenced
sliding into sleep

58

Swallows have those kind of eyes
world views to play with

Even in rain they are here
moving like the leaves do
in wind

Time is like that it seems
morning spirals that evolve
into day shapes
touching afternoons with evenings
towards night

life is that unfixed thing that takes
the many-sided patterns we create
to their fulfilment
or natural destruction
if that is right

Nothing is impossible
in words of God
but have we really seen the swallows
playing in the rain
with eyes that see
like ours do
and felt that soft pounding
on our wings

59

everything is here today
the flowers open-faced
the birds that sing unseen
in overlapping trees
the ordinary rocks that wait
exactly in their place
that scent
of earth, of leaves
the green air
of spring

none of this changes
as I unfold my thoughts
to wrap my day
tight in mindful games

all of life continues
centred in the moment
held in unvoiced identity
jigsawed into patterns
every piece
perfect and complete

60

between the stillness
of the sunlight
and the living space
we move in

one centre
one circle
and everything
within

a million raindrops
on the ocean

a single breath
upon the wind

one life
that never ends
so all this
can begin

61

the soft pulsating swirl
of peace
that spills out of any moment
held
in unmeasured contemplation

this is where
the daily joys
feed
the deepest roots
of the never ending
divine
contentment

every world has layers
that open to the touch
of senses
surrendered
in total
adoration

62

And at night
how many stars do we need
to be amazed
how many flowers
and how many colours
how many blackbirds
singing
even one song
how many hands
to be touched
or to hold
how many times
how many words
how long will we wait
to believe
that we are truly
here
to behold

Who knows
the last Spring
the final snowfall
that morning rose
scented with dew
that we will never
see again

63

nothing but this
wet stillness
dripping
jewelled raindrops
into my open hand

the sky is full of treasures
a million years of darkness
and then
a thousand miles of light
to wrap our little world
in clouds

here is where I stand
catching molten petals
as one by one
the clouds return
to Earth

64

snails
the whole world to explore
inch by inch
moment by moment
we are all
on the move

even trees are on a journey
that does not end
rocks are changing shape
and continents
are shifting

within the shell
the snail
is always totally
at home

each direction a spiral
of a thousand
new surprises

65

the sky today
the clouds
the ten thousand shapes
of thoughts
clothing everything
this tree   this branch   this leaf
is where it all begins

everything is named
and in its place

nothing changes
no time
no space

life and death
one movement
different shapes

the faded flower
curled
in fragile stillness
beauty changes form
every moment
uniquely
reborn

we recognise the signs
as step after step
moment within moment
the world is here
waiting
with her gifts

right now is when it all begins
everything included
with nothing left to reason
life is
exactly as she is

67

this duck's final call
at dusk
even birdsong
fades away
this day is laid to rest
nothing
to forgive
or regret

we are learning how to live
empty handed
naked to the past
fully stretched
every breath
releasing its fulness
embracing
the emptiness
every sense
caressing
this fleeting
living
presence

68

the day again
remembers
every leaf in place
a blackbird singing
and the song
rides the silence
end to end

even to a butterfly
living
flower to flower
life is what happens
nectar
or hunger
wings fold
and breathing
fades away

69

Once again
the mist of dawn
settles like diamonds
on the scattered grass

the trees
shadowless
drip pearls
of awakening light

Huddled deep
in these wet branches
eyes open
wings shuffle
and then
all words surrender

Only silence
can listen
to the stillness
where every song
begins

70

A thousand words of choices
to colour my day

and in between

the silence
of truth

that is the language
I listen for

the moment
when everything
has an equal voice

and time
has nothing left
to say

no beginning

no end